'Referendums, by their very nature, are conversations of nationhood.' So writes First Nations man Charles Prouse in this engaging Aboriginal storytelling-style essay about the Voice. Charles confronts the 'No' arguments sourced from both the dark place of Settler Australia's colonial prejudice and from the sovereignty warriors led by Senator Lidia Thorpe, and argues clearly why the Voice will benefit First Nations people and the Australian nation. It is a refreshingly honest essay from a First Nations man who understands complexity and how the story of constitutional recognition is just part of a long journey of restitution and justice.'

– Professor Peter Yu AM, Vice-President (First Nations), Australian National University

Charles Prouse is a Nyikina man from the Kimberley, Western Australia, with over 20 years' experience in Indigenous affairs across Australia. He holds a Master of Public Administration from Harvard University and a Bachelor of Science from the University of Western Australia. He has worked on Indigenous projects with state and federal governments and in the not-for-profit and private sectors, and co-owns NyikBar Consulting, specialising in supplier diversity and Indigenous program implementation. From 2015 to 2022 Charles was the first Indigenous person on the board of the Benevolent Society, and is Chair of the Aurora Education Foundation. He lives in Sydney.

Writers in the *On Series*

Fleur Anderson
Gay Bilson
John Birmingham
Chris Bowen
Julian Burnside
Blanche d'Alpuget
Paul Daley
Glyn Davis
Robert Dessaix
Juliana Engberg
Sarah Ferguson
Nikki Gemmell
Stan Grant
Germaine Greer
Sarah Hanson-Young
Jonathan Holmes
Mark Humphries
Daisy Jeffrey
Susan Johnson
Malcolm Knox
Barrie Kosky
Sally McManus
David Malouf
Paula Matthewson
Rick Morton
Katharine Murphy
Dorothy Porter
Amy Remeikis
Leigh Sales
Mark Scott
Tory Shepherd
Annika Smethurst
Tim Soutphommasane
David Speers
Natasha Stott Despoja
Anne Summers
Tony Wheeler
Evan Williams
Ashleigh Wilson
Elisabeth Wynhausen

Charles Prouse

On the Voice to Parliament

hachette AUSTRALIA

hachette
AUSTRALIA
Published in Australia and New Zealand in 2023
by Hachette Australia
(an imprint of Hachette Australia Pty Limited)
Gadigal Country, Level 17, 207 Kent Street, Sydney, NSW 2000
www.hachette.com.au

Hachette Australia acknowledges and pays our respects to the past, present and future Traditional Owners and Custodians of Country throughout Australia and recognises the continuation of cultural, spiritual and educational practices of Aboriginal and Torres Strait Islander peoples. Our head office is located on the lands of the Gadigal people of the Eora Nation.

A catalogue record for this book is available from the National Library of Australia

ISBN: 978 0 7336 5144 1 (paperback)

Cover design by Luke Causby, Blue Cork
Text design by Alice Graphics
Author photograph reproduced with the kind permission of the Benevolent Society
Uluru Statement from the Heart reproduced with the kind permission of regional dialogues and the Uluru National Constitutional Convention, May 2017
Typeset by Kirby Jones
Printed and bound in Australia by McPherson's Printing Group

'This isn't just one conversation – it's a lot of little conversations.'

– Aunty Heather

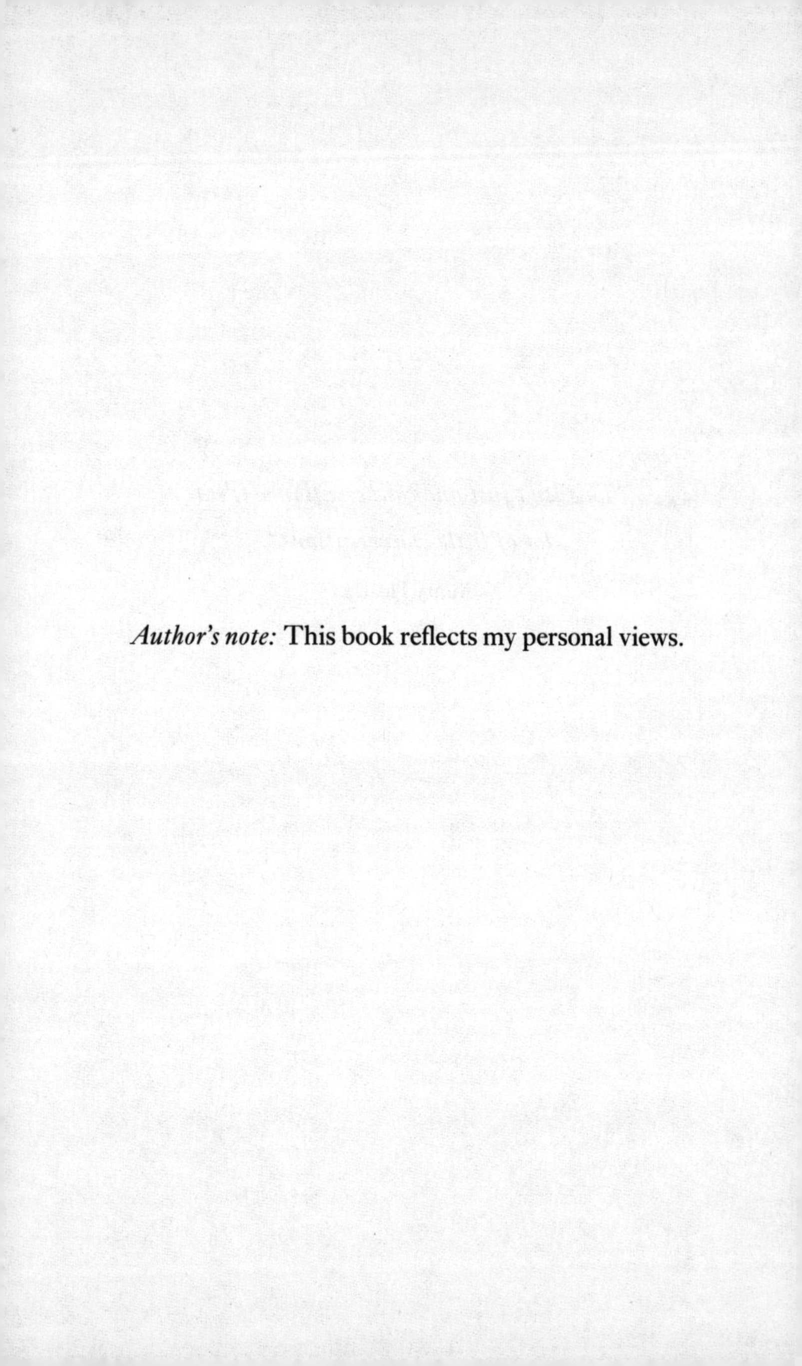

Author's note: This book reflects my personal views.

I am one Australian out of many. I'm proud to say I'm a First Nations Australian. I am a Nyikina man. My dad is Nyikina, so in our ways, I am Nyikina. My hometown is Derby in the Kimberley in Western Australia, which is surrounded by Nyikina country. My mum is Bardi and her Country (from Grandad) is about 150 kilometres away. Mum has blue coastal waters. Dad has muddy river/estuarine waters.

From Derby, the nearest town, Broome, is 220 kilometres away, on Yawuru Country. When I was growing up, a trip to Broome was a big adventure. As we got closer to Broome, the first sign we were arriving was seeing the tips of the sand dunes. We'd look out for them once we were about 10 kilometres away. That's what all the kids looked for. The dunes and the blue ocean were something exciting and different for a kid surrounded by bush and rivers. We were going to see our cousins and see their world – their Country. We loved it.

These days, to get home to Derby, I fly into Broome from Sydney. I still get excited by those blue waters, the dunes and the pindan, the red soil. Then another mini adventure awaits me when I get off the plane and do the 220-kilometre drive home. I am grateful to live on Gadigal land in Sydney, but I'm a proud Nyikina man with Bardi blood and Derby is always my home.

*

A book about the Voice to Parliament, 'the Voice'. The publisher says make it accessible so everybody can read it. It's for whoever wants to hear from an Aboriginal person about what they think of the Voice.

Who am I to speak about this? This is a national issue, an important issue, a complex issue. This Voice to Parliament is nationally important. Yes, it is about a minority of Australians. We're only 3 per cent of the Australian population according to Census data. And we're asking for the majority of Australians to support us.

This is no easy task. This is an issue of trust. Of hope. Of justice.

After decades of advocacy from First Nations leaders, our Prime Minister has put this on the national agenda. It is an issue of nationhood and the Prime Minister is asking us to have a conversation that is important for our future. That's their job. Guide us forward. Keep the country safe, don't muck it up. Keep us happy. Look after the place. Look after the people. We're only here for a short time. There are generations to come yet. We're all just passers-by in the big scheme of things. According to God, you have one life and you'd better use it wisely.

When people came from what some call 'the Mother Country', they talked to us about 'God', that God is in the stars, in the rocks; God is everywhere. We had the Dreaming before these people came. The Dreaming has guided Aboriginal people for over 60,000 years, and maybe God *is* the Dreaming.

I could never comprehend much of this. My mum says Father Lorenz dreaded teaching me in scripture classes because I asked so many questions about God and where all the fish came from at that big party and how Jesus could possibly walk on water. But for many of us blackfullas, we seem to have reconciled God and the Dreaming.

Our Dreaming tells us our history in story form, and from those stories come lessons. From lessons come learning and learning helps us survive – to look after ourselves and to look after Country. Otherwise, there is no future. There will be no land, water, plants or animals if we don't look after the place. If we don't look after the place there will be no kids to be born.

That might seem simplistic. I know a lot of us will be around in a year; in two years; probably even twenty. And we'll have kids. But it's getting harder to guarantee a safe environment – let alone one that is healthy and rich in biodiversity. Too many things lost. Too many animals lost. Too much fire. Too much rain.

It's a lot to contemplate. And maybe I'm not the person to talk about such things. However, we must all talk about them. Just like we must talk about this Voice to Parliament. Because this is a conversation for the whole country – for all of us.

*

I find myself now at 49 years of age, a gay black man living in Sydney. From Derby, where I was born and grew up, I've lived and worked in Derby, Perth, Melbourne, Derby again and now Sydney. My community, my work has always been in the world of Australian Indigenous issues. And I've gone home at least once a year, if not more. I stay as connected as I can to my family, my community, my Country. I hope that I can give a decent perspective as an Aboriginal person on this Voice to Parliament, and explain why it's important to vote Yes.

The Voice to Parliament proposal

The Voice to Parliament proposal has come from the Uluru Statement from the Heart. This statement was crafted over a number of days with a few hundred, mostly Indigenous, Australians, and made on 26 May 2017. It is the culmination of several years of consultations with First Nations people of Australia from around the country. The statement reads:

> Our Aboriginal and Torres Strait Islander tribes were the first sovereign Nations of the Australian continent and its adjacent islands, and possessed it under our own laws and customs. This our ancestors did, according to the reckoning of our culture, from the Creation, according to the common law from 'time immemorial', and according to science more than 60,000 years ago.

This sovereignty is a spiritual notion: the ancestral tie between the land, or 'mother nature', and the Aboriginal and Torres Strait Islander peoples who were born therefrom, remain attached thereto, and must one day return thither to be united with our ancestors. This link is the basis of the ownership of the soil, or better, of sovereignty. It has never been ceded or extinguished, and co-exists with the sovereignty of the Crown.

How could it be otherwise? That peoples possessed a land for sixty millennia and this sacred link disappears from world history in merely the last two hundred years?

With substantive constitutional change and structural reform, we believe this ancient sovereignty can shine through as a fuller expression of Australia's nationhood.

Proportionally, we are the most incarcerated people on the planet. We are not an innately criminal people. Our children are aliened from their families at unprecedented rates. This cannot be because we have no love for them. And our youth languish in detention in obscene numbers. They should be our hope for the future.

These dimensions of our crisis tell plainly the structural nature of our problem. This is the torment of our powerlessness.

We seek constitutional reforms to empower our people and take a rightful place in our own country. When we have power over our destiny our children will flourish. They will walk in two worlds and their culture will be a gift to their country.

We call for the establishment of a First Nations Voice enshrined in the Constitution.

Makarrata is the culmination of our agenda: the coming together after a struggle. It captures our aspirations for a fair and truthful relationship with the people of Australia and a better future for our children based on justice and self-determination.

We seek a Makarrata Commission to supervise a process of agreement-making between governments and First Nations and truth-telling about our history.

In 1967 we were counted, in 2017 we seek to be heard. We leave base camp and start our trek across this vast country. We invite you to walk with us in a movement of the Australian people for a better future.

I bring to our collective attention these lines: *We call for the establishment of a First Nations Voice enshrined in the Constitution.*

Makarrata is the culmination of our agenda: the coming together after a struggle. It captures our aspirations for a fair and truthful relationship with the people of Australia and a better future for our children based on justice and self-determination.

We seek a Makarrata Commission to supervise a process of agreement-making between governments and First Nations and truth-telling about our history.

It is here that the Uluru Statement from the Heart calls out to all Australians (not just the politicians) for three things:

- Voice
- Treaty
- Truth-telling

I'm going to talk about a First Nations Voice enshrined in the Constitution – 'the Voice'.

The Voice to Parliament is the first of these responses to the Uluru Statement. All Australians of voting age will be asked at a national referendum if they wish to amend modern Australia's foundational legal document.

Now the first thing I need to say is that we are *not* being asked to decide on a 'model' for what the Voice would look like. We need to separate the referendum question from what a proposed model might be. This is the first trap, and the main trap, in the debate, so let's focus on that. (There are lots of other traps in the referendum debate and I hope we call them out for what they are – traps and smokescreens – and some of them are outright lies. Maybe someone will write an essay on those.)

We are being asked whether we think Aboriginal and Torres Strait Islander people should be acknowledged as being a part of this country before it was colonised by the British and whether they should have a say about issues that affect them.

The legal wording of the proposed change to the Constitution is:

> A Proposed Law: to alter the Constitution to recognise the First Peoples of Australia by establishing an Aboriginal and Torres Strait Islander Voice.
>
> Do you approve this proposed alteration?

You may answer YES or NO. Abstaining is effectively the same as voting NO.

If the Australian people agree to this change in the referendum, a body called 'the Aboriginal and Torres Strait Islander Voice' will be set up. As stated by the National Indigenous Australians Agency (see the Appendix for more information), this Voice 'may make representations to the

Parliament and the Executive Government of the Commonwealth on matters relating to Aboriginal and Torres Strait Islander peoples'. This body will be able to speak to the Parliament (the politicians) and the executive arms of government (the department agencies and their executive management) about their policies and give advice on how they should be improved so we can get better outcomes for our First Nations brothers and sisters.

We've never done this properly before and this is the injustice we should try to fix. Nothing else has seemed to work. It's government policies that have caused so much wrong in our country, and every government has mucked this up. So let's set up this Voice and give Aboriginal and Torres Strait Islander people a position in this country where we don't have to fight every day for our existence. Through this, proper respect can be given to Australia's First Culture, our unique culture, in our modern nation.

Some people might worry that it will make our country worse. They worry about how it might affect *their* lives – rather than Aboriginal lives – we are only 3 per cent of the population, after all. So will this affect the rest of Australia in a good or bad way?

I would like to challenge all of us, especially non-Indigenous Australians, to think about how it might improve *your* life. For example, maybe you'll have a better relationship with your neighbours, your family; maybe it will make your kids happy because they want their Aboriginal friends to be happy – and that will make you happy.

Maybe there might be better infrastructure – in the bush! Aboriginal people need it, and so do other Aussies – those on stations and in regional and remote towns. Where are you, local government? Better infrastructure will help social harmony and attract people to live in these areas.

I won't unpack it for you – get informed and have the conversations. But please think about the positive things that could happen for you, for your work, for relationships with your Aboriginal neighbours. Because, at the moment, I'm being bombarded by negativity against the Voice (mostly smokescreens and disinformation) in the media. You must be too.

*

So back to setting up the Voice – if we vote Yes, the responsibility to set it up to Parliament will belong to the politicians we all elect. They can decide what it looks like and how many people are in it and how local and regional people are elected and all the other detail. And to help them, they do have a body of work, culminating in the Langton Calma report (see page 20), much of the lead-up to which was done with the close engagement of the Liberal and National Coalition.

Those same parties are now saying NO! Come on! Ken Wyatt, their minister who carried this process, the first Indigenous Minister in the Indigenous portfolio in this country, handed back his party membership in protest at his own party's decision against the Voice to Parliament. The Shadow Minister for Indigenous Australians, Julian Leeser, resigned from the front bench, saying he wanted to tell his kids he stood for something.

To those politicians who say it won't work, well, then – make it work, and continue to make it work as it evolves. That's why we elect you. You are not powerless.

All I hear from the No campaign is that there will be all these negative unintended consequences if we vote Yes. They don't talk about the unintended *good* consequences. They refuse to shift, no matter what. And down the track things might change, but hopefully they'll only continue to improve. And we'll learn. And we'll be better.

There's so much information about the Voice to Parliament, it can make you want to bury your head in the sand like an ostrich. But we're not ostriches – in Australia, we're emus, and emus are nosey things.

Since the Uluru Statement from the Heart was given as a declaration – an offering and a pathway forward for all Australians – appropriate responses continue to be developed and worked through. Of course, this kind of process takes a while.

So, where are we in the debate in the lead-up to this referendum? Here are the main points I've been hearing, reading, seeing, talking about:

- The consultation process wasn't done properly / I never got asked / Nobody spoke to me
- It's a Canberra model – made up by people in Canberra – not Aboriginal people out in the bush
- It's not going to elect the right people / I don't know how people are going to be elected so I don't trust it
- It's another ATSIC and that failed
- For us Aboriginal and Torres Strait Islander people, we'll be ceding our sovereignty
- We should have a treaty first
- It won't change anything – we need to close the gap

- It will divide us Aboriginal and Torres Strait Islander people
- It will divide Australians because it's racist *(tricky one, this – not because it's racist, but how to respond to this argument)*

So what happens if we vote YES?

Two widely respected Indigenous people, Professor Marcia Langton AO and Professor Tom Calma AO, co-chaired an advisory group and then wrote a 270-page report, called the 'Indigenous Voice Co-design Process Final Report to the Australian Government'. The report was the culmination of consultations, webinars, surveys, stakeholder meetings and written submissions that engaged more than 9400 people. From that engagement and with Professor Langton and Professor Calma's decades of experience, the report details the consultation and engagement process and presents considerations for implementing a Voice to Parliament.

I highly recommend that you read the report. That's what I did. That's what my mum did. And if you want the short version – read the executive summary.

But remember the first trap: it's a proposed 'model', it gives a lot of information on what the Voice to Parliament *might* look like if we vote Yes, and it will need further work. The report says so.

*

Earlier I said that a prime minister speaks to us about important issues. That's their job.

Well … our Prime Minister is doing his job – he is embracing the challenge of dealing with a great wrong in our country.

First, the Constitution needs amending in a way we can all live with.

If we vote Yes and give the Prime Minister the green light, then more work comes. He'll have the report, a body of work that's a seriously good starting point. Some people have complained about parts of it. But some people haven't read it. And all the problems people are pointing out (some are really silly) … well, the report recommends to keep consulting, which will address the criticisms about how this won't work or that won't work.

While the report is excellent, try not to get bogged down in the detail, and don't be fooled by lazy politicians and journalists who want to give us conflict and negativity. What have they done to help? It's so easy to pull something down. Being brave and building something for the future and making real change … now, that's leadership.

However, what the government won't be able to do – if we, the people, vote Yes to change the Constitution – is take away the voice of First Nations people. Once and for all, it will be acknowledged in our founding document that we have a special place in this country. Everyone might not agree on details, but we agree they should have been there in the first place and we acknowledge they should have a say about their lives.

The rest ... the rest we'll work through as a grown-up democracy.

We, the people, need to focus on the referendum question itself first.

An enormous amount of work has been done to provide the government and the general public information about what a *potential* Voice to Parliament might look like. Professors Langton and Calma have done the consultations and research and have experienced the reality of our community, organisational and political structures. They've had to engage Australia's ancient and first community and see how their practices and knowledge might work in a modern political system not designed for them.

This Voice mustn't threaten our country. It must make our country better, lifting up the most disadvantaged and, in doing so, lifting us all up.

The government has made a commitment to the Uluru Statement from the Heart – Voice, Treaty, Truth. The first part of that statement is Voice. The government is dealing with the Voice first with this referendum question. It will then deal with Treaty and Truth.

I hope that in the lead-up to and on the day of the referendum we are thinking of these questions:

- Should Aboriginal and Torres Strait Islander people be given a voice in the land they've been a part of for more 60,000 years? They have been excluded in our founding document – is that correct?
- Should we be a better country and look after our ancient heart?
- Should we finally address the massive injustice our country has been built upon and do it properly – in the Constitution document that sets the fundamental rules for us, and which is meant to define us and should be unique to Australia?
- Can we look to the future with hope and compassion?

As mentioned earlier, further consultation will be required on the issues people are worried about – and many of these are addressed in the report.

Everyone deserves their questions addressed on something so fundamental to the future of our society. Deciding to vote Yes will kick-start a change that will improve our nation collectively. And so, we have the Langton Calma report on what a legislative model might look like if we vote Yes. But the questions of whether the Voice will be deciding our military capabilities or the notion that somehow it will bring our country to some kind of grinding halt are born out of fear and laziness.

*

There will be standards that guide the Voice on what it will and won't focus on. It will speak to the particular policies that have not worked for us – that have been designed without true appreciation of our 'situation'. There will be timeframes for the Voice to work within so government doesn't come to a grinding halt. And there won't be any kind of veto power. We're only asking to be heard.

We'll make our case for improvement on policies, with data and evidence. We aren't here to make things worse – in fact, things couldn't get any worse for us. We want to make life better. Making life better for First Nations people doesn't make life worse for everyone else. Making life better for us *with all Australians* makes life better *for all of us.* Better education for everyone, better integration of our ancient culture for everyone, better health and infrastructure that will make our country better, our society better.

We just want a job, a roof over our head, a reason to live, to be happy, to be truly included and given an acknowledgement that we were here first. We've been ignored, killed and broken because you think you know what's better for us. And it's not right. It's not working.

As a first step, I urge you to read the report. Or just read the executive summary. But remember the trap – we're not being asked to vote on the report/the model. We're being asked if a Voice should exist. The report should give you comfort that a lot of exceptional work has been done and is a great starting point. The politicians will need to do their job and improve upon it if the people think it needs more work. Don't let them off the hook.

*

So with that in mind, I'd like to introduce my mother, Iris Prouse. Mum and I talk a lot about Aboriginal politics. A while back, she said to me, 'Charles, I read that report, you know, and it's pretty good. It explains it for me.'

Then she told me she watched shows on ABC iView like Q&A and heard speakers on the radio and watched people, such as Senator Lidia Thorpe, on the TV. I might have been the first in our family to go to university, but my mother has always set the tone regarding knowledge-seeking, doing the work and getting to the heart of a matter (and, yes, I might be biased, but you'd be hard-pressed to find a person who doesn't respect her wisdom).

The report tells you how the consultations were done across the country, especially in regional and remote Australia. People at the meetings in regional and remote areas wanted to be sure that those at the grassroots were represented on this national body called the Voice to Parliament, and they wanted regional approaches and regional solutions. So, no, it's not a 'Canberra Voice'.

*

There's the government website on the Voice to Parliament – pamphlets, factsheets, posters and diagrams abound! The ABC has a thirteen-minute video about the Voice to Parliament, and I'm sure there's a podcast out there. Just don't be an ostrich and bury your head in the sand – be an inquisitive Aussie emu!

Why do we need to change the Constitution?

Some say that we should test the Voice to Parliament through legislation first before we enshrine it in the Constitution. The problem with that approach is that it has already been tried. The Aboriginal and Torres Strait Islander Commission (ATSIC) was established in 1990 by the Hawke Government as an Australian government agency responsible for representing and advocating for the rights and welfare of Aboriginal and Torres Strait Islander people. Its main purpose was to empower Indigenous Australians by involving them in the decision-making process regarding policies and programs that directly affected their communities. ATSIC was comprised of regionally elected representatives of Aboriginal and Torres Strait Islander people. Those regional representatives then elected a national Commission, who in turn provided advice to Canberra, its ministers and its bureaucrats. It was dismantled by the Howard Government in 2004 and formally abolished in 2005.

I worked for ATSIC as a junior. I started on reception, then I became a junior project officer. It was one of my first jobs during my university holidays. I was studying in Perth and when I went home to Derby, I'd work at ATSIC if there was an opportunity. It was where I learned more about our system of government, how it was connected to our people. There were regional, state and national election processes for our people that gave us some control over our own lives. I saw Aboriginal managers, learned what policy was and that Aboriginal and Torres Strait Islander people were writing policy. That policy was then put into funding guidelines and if the community needed funds to support its programs, it had to fill out funding applications that met policy guidelines.

The policy guidelines were written by Aboriginal people who knew what the challenges were and knew what outcomes were needed.

ATSIC did not fund major areas such as health and education which are the responsibility of governments. It funded the Community Development and Education Projects (CDEP) and the Community Housing and Infrastructure Program (CHIP). In the Appendix there's a link to the Australian Parliament's comprehensive report on the history of ATSIC, its funding, its governance and 'its successes and failures, both real and perceived'.

This report states that CDEP was 'an employment, training, and community development program that began in 1977, providing work and training opportunities for unemployed Indigenous people in community-based and community-managed activities. In June 2002, there were over 270 Indigenous community organisations and 34,182 Indigenous people participating in CDEP nationally.'

CHIP funded 'a variety of projects, ranging from the construction and acquisition of appropriate rental housing for Indigenous people, to providing adequate water, power and sewerage supplies to rural and remote Indigenous communities. The services provided with CHIP funding vary depending on the community's location and the mainstream services already available.'

And then there were the activities centring on our culture, heritage and our sense of community – such as youth programs, festivals, language programs and women's shelters.

You'll note the repeated use of the word 'community' – community development, community housing, programs for the community. And community is what I saw and experienced and it made me feel good. It left its mark on me. I know the value of community. I was employed as an Aboriginal person by my community (yes, in a government department but it was my community in that department) to be on the ground and speak with my community when they came through the door, to support a community program funded by our region for the kids to practise culture through art, music, language or support a community or sporting festival. I was happy, the community was happy, the kids were happy, and their parents were happy that their kids were happy.

Something died again for me when ATSIC was taken from us. Our community took yet another blow. Without a central point like ATSIC, which concerns us and how our culture works and helps us celebrate who we are and honours our community ways, life for Aboriginal people has deteriorated.

Some might say that First Nations people rely on government too much. I wish we didn't have to. But the government, its systems and its changing of policies with new politicians has been the fundamental cause of our problems and the constant issues we need to deal with to get our basics sorted – justice, health, housing and Caring for Country.

Did ATSIC do that? Well … no. It wasn't designed to truly fix all those issues. It was never given a fair hearing. It was fighting an uphill battle on an hourly basis. But the community activities kept us connected. Women's shelters were supported by the community, and you can say what you like about CDEP, but it was run by Indigenous people for Indigenous people and it kept an eye on and gave support to young people in a way that worked. There are foundations there that are still being used today. There are success stories from CDEP.

Then there's the argument that ATSIC mismanaged funds. Well, going from being a young university student to a person who has worked across government, the non-profit sector and with a few of our biggest national and global companies, I can confidently say the ATSIC money was paltry. Costs included staffing, leases, travel, events, equipment, consultants, contractors … the list goes on. There was an internal audit unit and ATSIC was accountable to the Parliament by means of the tabling of a formal annual report. So the money was accounted for.

It appalls me that governments make broad statements saying that ATSIC was a failure and mismanaged funds. Then journalists who want to feed the public 'bad news' stories carry that message through and don't interrogate the real situation. When I hear members of the general public say ATSIC was a failed experiment, my heart both sinks and hardens because they've repeated the same lazy politicians' words, backed up by journalists who don't explain the full story.

I say to them (in the context of ATSIC), try walking in our shoes, then deal with the policy headaches, the funding headaches, the historical and ongoing trauma and racism the community wants you to address, set up systems and processes and guidelines, engage with everyone from the Aunty who needs a chair at the festival to give her comfort from her aching foot caused by diabetes, to the local member, the state member, the federal member – write that position paper, go to this national or state conference – and don't forget that local government meeting and the school parents' meeting and deal with your staff who are part of the community, who have the pain and trauma just like you do (oh, and deal with that while you're at it). ATSIC was not a failed experiment. It was dealing with 'the situation' (you know … the 'Aboriginal situation' that some people ask me about, wanting to know how it can be fixed).

ATSIC had limited capacity to deal with these issues and were expected to engage with everyone on everything. Other departments had tight mandates; years of institutional processes and practices defined by and for non-Indigenous Australians and few of them had to engage the community at the most local of levels consistently across a nation that's expensive to get around. ATSIC had to engage with the proverbial every person and his dog in a melting pot of languages and cultural practices that were old before Captain Cook came. Then ATSIC was not given a fair hearing when it was criticised for not meeting the white man's unfair expectations to fix something the white man broke.

Without ATSIC, there is no anchor to keep us together; we are adrift. The divide-and-conquer tactic has been, and continues to be, used against us.

The problem with abolishing ATSIC was that it was equivalent to abolishing our First Nations voice. It was a model where we had elections run by the Australian Electoral Commission, but it was legislated and not in the Constitution. The government of the day could abolish it without consultation if they had the numbers – and they did.

As for the scandals, the alleged misuse of funds ... it wasn't *all* of ATSIC and our people. How many other government agencies have been engulfed by scandal? Have all our politicians been squeaky clean? If they haven't, should we do away with parliament? Have we done away with the government agencies that threw good money after bad? Why couldn't we have had a review of ATSIC and a restructure? No – the government's response was to punish all of us by denying our voices.

*

A legislative approach has been tried and failed. Without it being embedded in the Constitution, our voice can be taken away by any government of the day at any time. Embedding a Voice in the Constitution will make it much more difficult for any government to simply de-legislate any kind of institution that speaks for the Aboriginal and Torres Strait Islander community. We would like to be heard as a matter of principle – as First Nations people of this country – regardless of who is in power. That is the principle we would like. We would like to be heard.

We have a right to be heard. After 60,000 years of custodianship; after 230 years and generations of suffering; after being murdered, poisoned, raped, having our land stolen and even being denied as citizens for 67 years since the federation of this modern nation, we continue to pay in blood for a special place in the Constitution. We should be recognised – more, we need to be heard. We should have a say in our lives. The First Nations people of this land would like to be heard so we can strengthen ourselves; so we can strengthen the spirit of this country; so we can regenerate ourselves, this land and, in the process, regenerate this nation for all Australians into a better and stronger country.

We are not saying we want to 'take over' anything – there's no way we can. We just want a say in our lives.

I'm proud of this country and I'm proud of my connection to it, but my parents have suffered; my family has suffered; my nephews and nieces have suffered. They still suffer. I worry that they will end up in the gaol system.

It's time for things to change.

Challenging the idea of the Voice

There are those who are yet to give support to the Voice to Parliament. I agree with some things they say. For example, I agree with Senator Lidia Thorpe when she talks about implementing the recommendations of the Bringing Them Home report and the Deaths in Custody report in full. She's right – it has been too long since those reports were tabled. For more than 25 years we have been waiting for the full implementation of both reports. But it is the various state and territory governments who must do this. After more than two decades (three decades for the Deaths in Custody report), state and territory governments of all political persuasions have failed to fully implement the recommendations, and they should all hang their heads in shame for not doing so. It is the laws of those states and territories in relation to justice, child protection, education and housing that must be addressed. Aboriginal people are used in the game of political football where each party blames the other for not doing something.

The Bringing Them Home report

The Bringing Them Home report was the result of a national inquiry conducted by the Australian Human Rights and Equal Opportunity Commission (now known as the Australian Human Rights Commission) from 1995 to 1997. Sir Ronald Wilson and Mick Dodson led that process.

The report examined the forced removal and separation of Aboriginal and Torres Strait

Islander children from their families, commonly known as the Stolen Generations. The Stolen Generations era refers to the policies and practices that were implemented by Australian governments from the mid-1800s to the 1970s, which aimed to assimilate Indigenous children into white society by removing them from their families, communities and culture.

The Bringing Them Home report documented the personal testimonies of those affected by these removal policies, including Indigenous individuals, families and communities. It shed light on the traumatic experiences, the devastating consequences and the ongoing intergenerational impacts of these policies on Indigenous Australians. I have a copy of the report on my bookshelf. I have to put it down after reading any individual testimony. What happened was horrific and shocking, and I need to recover from the gut-wrenching sensations that threaten to overwhelm me as I read people's personal accounts of their trauma.

The report made several important findings and recommendations, including acknowledging the historical and ongoing effects of the removal policies, apologising to the Stolen Generations, providing reparations and compensation, supporting healing and reconciliation processes and promoting Indigenous self-determination.

A National Apology was finally given to the Stolen Generations by then-Prime Minister Kevin Rudd in 2008. I was on the lawn of Parliament House in Canberra with thousands of others. I'm sure millions of Australians remember where they were. Many people – Indigenous and non-Indigenous – told me it felt like a unifying moment for the nation and many felt proud to be Australian in that moment.

But there are still issues from the report that state and territory governments have struggled to implement effectively. And the number of Indigenous children in out-of-home care (foster care) has drastically increased in the last decade.

The Australian Institute of Health and Welfare released a report showing that 18,862 Indigenous kids were in out-of-home care in 2020. This was eleven times the rate for non-Indigenous children according to Catherine Liddle, the CEO of the Secretariat of National Aboriginal and Islander Child Care (SNAICC).

According to AbSec, the New South Wales equivalent of SNAICC, more than 6600 Aboriginal children were in statutory out-of-home care as of 30 June 2020. This is an increase of approximately 1100 Aboriginal children from 30 June 2016.

We are still going downhill!

The Bringing Them Home report emphasised the importance of Indigenous self-determination and called for increased Indigenous participation in decision-making processes regarding policies and programs that affect us – sound similar to a Voice to Parliament?

The Deaths in Custody report

The final report of the Royal Commission into Aboriginal Deaths in Custody, often referred to as the Deaths in Custody report, was published in 1991. The commissioners included Patrick Dodson – dubbed the Father of Reconciliation. The Royal Commission was established to investigate the causes and circumstances surrounding the deaths of Aboriginal and Torres Strait Islander individuals while in custody, including police custody, prisons and juvenile detention centres.

The report examined 99 cases of Indigenous deaths in custody that occurred between 1980 and 1989 and provided detailed analysis of the contributing factors and systemic issues, as well as recommendations for preventing future deaths. It highlighted issues such as over-policing, inappropriate use of force, inadequate healthcare, cultural insensitivity and systemic racism within the justice system.

The Deaths in Custody report is important for several reasons:

1. *Highlighting systemic issues:* the report exposed the disproportionate rates of Indigenous incarceration, the mistreatment and neglect experienced by Indigenous individuals in custody and the need for systemic reforms.

2. *Calls for justice and accountability:* it called for thorough investigations, fair trials and appropriate disciplinary actions against those responsible for any wrongdoing.
3. *Recommendations for change:* the report made comprehensive recommendations aimed at addressing the underlying causes of Indigenous deaths in custody, including areas such as law enforcement practices, access to justice, healthcare provision, cultural awareness training and community engagement.
4. *Influence on policy and advocacy:* the report played a significant role in shaping policy discussions and advocacy efforts related to Indigenous rights and criminal justice reform in Australia. It contributed to ongoing efforts to reduce Indigenous

> incarceration rates, improve conditions in custody and promote Indigenous self-determination.

My firm belief is that since the release of the report, state and territory governments of all political persuasions have failed dismally to respond to the full suite of recommendations. Yes, there are some justice programs and some cultural awareness, but really ... all governments have yet to address all the issues. There have been 547 Indigenous deaths in custody since the Royal Commission. That's in addition to the 99 that were investigated nearly 30 years ago.

Since those reports, we continue to languish in gaol, there are more kids in gaol and more Aboriginal and Torres Strait Islander children are being taken into out-of-home care than ever before. Senator Thorpe is right to call for the full implementation of those report recommendations. And in those reports is the call for the self-determination and the need for Indigenous people to be part of the decision-making process in issues affecting our lives. The reports aren't separate to a Voice to Parliament. We need a Voice to Parliament. And we need those reports' recommendations to be implemented. We need both.

The proposed Voice model is based on self-determination. Regional representation is required first, in order for a national Voice to be established and thus be given legitimacy by the regions. And it is in the regions where the work will take place – local people providing local solutions. (Check out the executive summary of the Langton Calma report, see the Appendix for how to find it online.) I know I'm repeating myself, but it's important to remember that the processes can and will be improved upon, as the report says.

Since many of the recommendations around the Bringing Them Home report are state and territory government issues, it would be the local/regional structures of the Voice model that could hold these governments to account, and they in turn would work with the federal government when they elect their own people to sit on the Voice to Parliament. The proposed Voice to Parliament model allows for regional influence (in fact, demands it) to get the recommendations of the Bringing Them Home and Deaths in Custody reports implemented – finally.

A Treaty

Senator Thorpe has also called for a Treaty. I agree with her on that, too. Australia is the only Commonwealth nation that does not have a treaty with its First Nations people. The Uluru Statement talks about Voice, Treaty, Truth. We need the Voice first. The Voice will help us organise ourselves for discussions with the Australian government, and it will represent us to the Australian government to negotiate a Treaty. If we're concerned about the order (which I firmly believe is the right order), and we say no to a Voice, then who's going to negotiate a Treaty – a representative group of all our Nations? (Wouldn't that start to look like a Voice?) But again, I say, we want a Treaty. No one is saying we don't. Let's get the Voice happening first.

We can then focus on the Treaty and Truth-telling processes through the regional structures of the Voice to Parliament. In going through those regional processes, we'll be able to have an open and honest dialogue on what a Treaty should start to look like.

I've chosen to discuss some of the big issues I felt that Senator Thorpe has raised, as I see them. I'd now like to turn to the other big issue that, since I started writing this, has become a major talking point on this referendum question – the topic of racism. Some say that the referendum is set to divide Australians, including Aboriginal and Torres Strait Islander people, based on race.

The Voice and racism

I asked two people for their thoughts when I was writing this essay. First, I asked a close friend, Jason Glanville, proud Wiradjuri man and Indigenous governance expert.

And I asked my mother in Derby. Powerful woman – don't mess with her. We never did. We weren't game to.

*

Jason, what do you have to say about people who say the Voice is racist, that it sets up one minority group? That we're asking a majority to give a minority a power based on race, and that's racist. And our Constitution should be devoid of racism?

As we've discussed before, Charles, the Constitution already is fundamentally racist because of the race power* – it gives Parliament the power to make special laws on behalf of a particular race. It's not specifically an Indigenous power, but it has been weaponised against us in the past and continues to be. It's a great shame that we weren't able to tackle that, the removal of that provision, as part of the referendum. But I understand that it's too much. We can't always walk and chew gum at the same time, particularly with something as complex as the Constitution.

But, fundamentally, the entire policy apparatus that has too much influence on the lives of our families and communities is racist because of that provision and others in the law that allow policymakers and politicians to make special consideration for blackfullas. And what I think the Voice attempts to do is start to level the playing field. But it doesn't even really do that. There's no authority or power in it in terms of compelling a response from government. It's the capacity to raise our collective voice on issues that matter. It doesn't tackle racism, but it certainly isn't in and of itself racist – the history of us being silenced and excluded is what is racist.

I like your point about levelling the playing field. And, in a sense, it's about putting us in a document that we should have always been in.

There is this ridiculous idea that the Voice elevates us above everybody else. We've never had the same status or opportunity, you know, community by community, individual by individual, family by family. People have risen up despite all the odds against Aboriginal people. So this idea that it gives us more, or allows us a different set of rights, it's just not true. It's getting us one step closer to some kind of equal form of rights.

Mum has said, people who say the Voice is all about racism, well, that's just lazy. That's a lazy argument. We can't move forward if it's just given the label of 'racism'. So that's the end of the conversation. Well, it's not.

No, that argument is a dog-whistle based on fear, which is the heart of what racism is. Racism's just about fear. And I don't think the majority of these people are genuinely fearful of how we'll use the Voice. They're fearful of what they'll lose. They think that any kind of advancement for Aboriginal people means they have to give something up. And history shows that it's actually to the benefit of all Australians. Improving the outcomes for blackfullas led by Aboriginal people will make a difference. It will be better for GDP and better for social harmony. It will be better for the sense of who we are as a country.

It's a nation-building exercise.

Thanks Jas.

* NOTE: Jason is talking about section 51(xxvi) of the Constitution, which gives Parliament the power to make special laws on behalf of a particular race. (See the Appendix for links to information about the race power.)

It was the use of the race power in 2007 that enabled the Howard Government to suspend the *Racial Discrimination Act*, then go into the Northern Territory and take control of the daily lives of Aboriginal people. Imagine the government sending the army into your community and requiring everyone to have medical check-ups. That went on for a few years, took away many of the freedoms most Australians take for granted and put families and kids through trauma no one would think is acceptable in a modern democracy in the 21st century. And it was done with hardly any notice, hardly any consultation with local people, and you could hear the unsaid, 'We're doing this for your own good because we know better.'

*

Earlier I mentioned how I often talk about Aboriginal politics with my mum, Iris. She has only recently retired. She's earned it. She's worked with our community all her life – in the professional sense, it's been over fifty years. Mum worked for Kimberley Community Health and then Environmental Health in the Kimberley and is a well-respected member of the community. She was a shire councillor for the Shire of Derby for twenty years and was the Environmental Health Manager for seventeen years. As well as that, she was on the Aboriginal Students' Parents Association for five years – with five of us at school, she wanted to do her bit to make sure we were getting a good education. Mum is from a family of eleven and my grandparents were also well-respected Kimberley people.

So when I was thinking of someone I could discuss some more questions about the Voice with, I really couldn't go past my mother.

I really don't know what I'm going to ask you, Mum. I'll just tell you where I'm at. We've tried the legislative process and it can be taken away. The Constitution is a series of principles and base laws. It's not the detail. So the Constitution does not tell us how to elect our prime minister. The Constitution does not tell us about how to structure our High Court or any of our federal agencies. So I don't think people should be caught up with that and go down the rabbit warren of the detail of the model at this point.

Yes, that's right, you can adapt, you can frame it, you can regionalise it. But the principle is having a voice, having the ability to advocate, influence, make recommendations, put suggestions on the table, start a dialogue. We would have the ability to do that. There would be a starting point.

At the moment, the only representation we have is the people that we elect to parliament. And they don't represent just Aboriginal people. They represent the region. And they'll leave parliament one day – other people will be elected – and we don't know if they'll be Indigenous or if they'll advocate for us.

And what do you say to people who say, well, the Voice is racist. You know, you are giving up too much power. The referendum is asking the majority to give power to a minority, and people are now saying because it's based on race, that it's racist.

Well, welcome to my world! You know, to us, isn't what's happened, and continues to happen to us, racist? The Constitution was racist. It didn't accept us until 1967. We grew up with that – I grew up with that. And there was the assumption that we, we had to accept it, on our Country. Where we originated from, we were told to accept this colonialism that Captain Cook brought across with him.

And now are we guilty of the same thing?

No, I don't think we're guilty of that. You can have racism everywhere, but to me, saying the Voice is racist, that's a cop-out, that's a generalised statement.

To me, it seems people are scared, people are frightened. It's the unknown. They don't know how this is going to turn out.

And what do you say to that, then?

Well, Charles, you'll never know until you actually try it. You'll never know.

And what's worse? What's the worst that could happen?

Exactly. What's the worst that can happen? Do we just say no? Because that's the safe way. Make no changes. Keep things the same as we've always had. But look at how that's working for us. It's not. It's shocking.

And, look, it's not going to split our people.

Split Aboriginal people or our country?

Some people, particularly the ones in the No camp, are saying it'll split our people. It'll split us more. But, look, it's already happening, Charles. We're already split.

Our mob, our kids. Aboriginal elders are now speaking out about what's happening with the younger generation. Current policies and practices are already causing a split. The BasicsCard, that's causing a split; alcohol restrictions, they're causing a split. So where do you start and where do you stop?

So do people just do nothing and we go back into a fetal position and just hope someone else will save us?

Exactly. Someone else will come along. And we'll get that dictatorship. That dictatorship will continue, Charles.

We are trying to save ourselves.

I think it's the unknown, Charles. That's what scares people. We're going into uncharted waters.

Well, yeah. But we've also been doing this for 230-something years. Uncharted waters. And it's gone nowhere. We've been in the deep, surrounded by sharks, for centuries now. We're looking for a lifeline. Will someone help us? Because we're trying to help ourselves, the debate about whether you should take the lifeline or not, or stay in the deep with the sharks. I'm not one to stay in the deep with the sharks, myself.

And we're ready. We've got people, Aboriginal people that are coming through universities. We've got Aboriginal CEOs; we've got leadership already out there. But they face entrenched institutional racism themselves – you do! I want them to speak up more. I want to hear their voice.

Well give them a voice. I suppose that's the thing. People might say, well, if you've got those

> *CEOs and those academics and whatever, do you really need the Voice?*
>
> If we get the Yes vote, we can mould it to whatever shape we want it to be. Yes. We do have CEOs out there, but CEOs are governed by a board and who sits on those boards? Yes. We do have our lawyers, our doctors but there's still a layer of management that sits above them. And we will have our disputes, just watch Question Time in Parliament. If you guys can't get it right, why are you expecting us to get it wrong?

*

Mum and I talked about how this notion that you have to survive as an individual has not helped us. Not for 250 years. That's not our way. The white man's way has not helped us, the white man has put his ways and his ideas and his attitude and his thinking on top of us without asking us, without caring about us. He's put it in the way that he wants it, not how we want it.

'History reflects that, Charles,' Mum said, and I wholeheartedly agree. We have always gone with how the white man wants it.

Is the Voice racist? No. It's equity. We deserve our say.

'Well, you can call it racist, we call it equity,' Mum said. 'To me, saying, "You're a racist", that's a cop-out, Charles. I don't want to hear that. Come up with something other than just that's "racist".'

Yeah. That's an easy one.

To people who say the Voice proposal is racist, Mum says – 'Tell the kid who was knocked down by the policeman that the Voice is racist. It's racist when the policeman comes in and shoots that boy and then goes on leave on full pay and doesn't go to gaol himself. Tell the mother who's had her baby taken away that the Voice is racist.'

That's racism.

'Using the word "racism" to shut down a conversation, then walking away because that's the end of the conversation, isn't right. We have to challenge that. If we can stop saying things like that, then we're on the way to having a united front. Both sides should be one side. We are trying for one side. We really are, we are trying so hard for one side.'

Mum has the ability to get it just right. And the two of us can talk … and talk.

She said, 'Sometimes it's our own people who have set themselves up as gatekeepers. Will some of that power be gone for them? Do they object to the Voice because people might no longer look up to them or seek them out? And this is the point. We're trying NOT to give the few power, we're trying to give the people on the frontline their voice. You want to know about education? Then talk to someone in education. You want to know about justice? Then talk to someone in justice. Talk to them because they're the experts and they're the ones that are at the coalface. But the reason why you won't often get to talk to them is because they're out there doing their jobs. Don't just talk to the person who thinks he or she knows everything. Because they don't.'

As a collective, we can support each other. At the moment, we don't have the ability to do that.

Mum saying much the same as she's done many times in the past always makes my heart drop. We've talked for years about how sad the situation is for our people. We've had innovation and success, sure, but it's always been a battle for us since colonisation.

'Things aren't right with our people,' she said. 'So do we accept the status quo? Or will we make some sort of attempt to change it, modify it, shape it so that this doesn't continue? Or do we just sit back on our hands and say No? Don't we have to do something? You know, the gap isn't closing. It's widening.'

She went on to say, 'We've got some of our youth who have no respect. They're running amok, you know – we've got people who just won't work and some are too sick to work.

'So what's the government's response? Legislation. Forced work for pay, the BasicsCard. So young kids coming through feel their world is limited, stacked against them. You MUST do this, you MUST do that. Why are we constantly using the stick approach and always coming from a place of negativity?

'We need to change this attitude of negativity that we are seeing; always looking at non-Indigenous leaders and policymakers, who are always looking at us through a deficit lens. We need to change it, particularly for the young generations – we need to cut our kids some slack. It's not their fault. The previous generations, we could have done better, but we've been victims of policy and legislative failure.'

I think to myself how unbelievably appalling this is, and am reminded of things I witnessed in my childhood, in my teenage years and into young adulthood.

I've seen shop managers take carved boab nuts (they're works of art that take hours to carve) from community people who had no money – for a few cans of beer. Those boab nuts sell for over $50. I've seen drug use seep into our community and grow more severe in time. I've seen the ongoing effects of those drugs added to the already dangerous levels of alcohol consumption that tear our families apart. I've seen a man kick and punch a woman down the street in broad daylight. I've seen what that does to the next generation – fetal alcohol syndrome, unstable home environments, poor school attendance and dismal education outcomes. It's grown worse in the last ten years.

I've seen it in my work. I've seen attempts to address the problem, like the Closing the Gap Framework, that have hardly helped us. There are now seventeen targets where the Commonwealth and the states are meant to work together and reduce the gap in outcomes between Indigenous and non-Indigenous

Australians. But most of the targets are not on track for the gaps to be closed. For example, some of the targets we're not meeting are:

- By 2031, increase the proportion of Aboriginal and Torres Strait Islander babies with a healthy birthweight to 91 per cent. *Improving but not on track.*
- By 2031, increase the proportion of Aboriginal and Torres Strait Islander people (age 20–24) attaining Year Twelve or equivalent qualification to 96 per cent. *Improving but not on track.*

I could go on, but here's one of the most terrible ones:

- By 2031, significant and sustained reduction in suicide of Aboriginal and

> Torres Strait Islander people towards zero. *Not on track and worsening.*

These have come from the government's own data. And while you can find this on the current Labor government Indigenous Australians Minister's website, the Liberal government was in power for nine years – up until last year. These statistics didn't arise just when Labor won the federal election in 2022. But all state and territory governments, be they Liberal or Labor, don't have any right to be happy with their achievements.

My mother says, 'Our kids need help. Their parents need help. The way of the individual is not working. Let's try a community approach. Let's try our community approach to fix this horrible situation. You can say all you like that they should go study at university and stand on their own two feet and they should learn how to manage a bank account and all of that. We are telling you it's not working. We're telling you give us community and family power and we might be able to do something as a collective.'

Mum's deep feeling is that we can't just sit on our hands and do nothing. And she's not saying that the Voice is the whole answer, but it's the first step. That was recognised at Uluru, and encapsulated in the Uluru Statement.

She says it's a cycle and we have to break that cycle. We can't do nothing. If the No vote gets up, what do we do? Do we continue to let the same people who say No influence policy because that's their job and they don't want that role given to somebody else? Well, it's not working. When they go, what kind of legacy will be left? We need to set up something that lasts the test of time.

It was late, so we wound up the conversation. She said she was crossing fingers, crossing everything, for the Yes vote. If there is a Yes vote, she hopes the people against the Voice will accept it and work with it even though they didn't agree with it. That they will try to make it work.

I hope the Australian people will say that they want this. That something has to give, and they will vote on the principle. Then we can all make it work because it's what's right. It's what Aboriginal and Torres Strait Islander people need.

'It's the right thing to do. We have an opportunity. We need to make it work.'

Mum's right, as usual.

*

I'll take it further and ask you to look beyond – not with the suspicion of someone having more power than you, and not with worry, but with bravery and hope.

Cathy Freeman winning gold at the Sydney Olympics was a unifying moment – when she ran with both the Australian national flag and the Aboriginal flag despite being warned it would be divisive. It was exactly the opposite – it was a momentous occasion for all Australians. Our hearts, our liyan – our spirit, our sense of wellbeing – swelled with pride and hope for tomorrow for us as a nation.

Our Constitution did not recognise us as equal to other Australians in its first 67 years. Finally, our country took the step to count us as Australian citizens. Australia finally acknowledged the devastating impact of decades of forced child removal laws when Prime Minister Rudd led the country and gave the National Apology in 2008.

Some people declared that these moments would bring impending doom for the nation. But all the 'sky falling' warnings that were given by those who told us not to take a risk, not to look beyond the here and now, did not come to pass. Instead bravery was chosen, our humanity was given the opportunity to shine and we took it, and we've basked in that glow of collective compassion and hope for the future.

Those historical moments didn't fix the problem, though – it's still here. Our country needs to be brave again.

*

These conversations with my brother-boy, Jason, and my mum help me. They help me unpack the issues in my head as I see them and check to see if they make sense. Of course I spoke with like-minded people. I didn't speak with Senator

Thorpe or others with a view different from mine. But I have tried to listen and read about what they've had to say. I remain in the Yes camp because I believe in the principle of being heard.

The entire Uluru Statement from the Heart is a statement of beauty and eloquence. Those who crafted it did so from lived experience. There was disagreement by some but the majority supported it. We are not a homogenous people – we have differences of opinion. But I firmly believe that in the crafting of the words, thoughts were not given to the self or even to the present alone. The words in the Statement come from an ancient past, centre us in the present and look to the future for all of us as a nation. For all Aboriginal and Torres Strait Islander people – young, old, country, city – connected to each other, not by native title laws, pieces of paper or how much language you speak, but by an ancient and familial bond, no matter how frayed. Our spirit – our liyan – will always be strong. This was, and always will be, Aboriginal and Torres Strait Islander land.

Our Country is not reconciled. There is a deep injustice here. And we are trying to fix it. Can we all fix it?

Try not to look at this Voice to Parliament with worry and fear in your heart – embrace bravery and hope.

*

Referendums, by their very nature, are conversations of nationhood. This referendum is not one single conversation. This essay doesn't deal with all the issues. This is my small sharing of thoughts, generously added to by my friend and my mum. And I'll give the last quote to one of my mum's sisters, Aunty Heather, who said to me: 'Charles, I don't think it's just one conversation – it's a lot of little conversations.'

And so another voice is added to the mix.

We all need to keep talking – at home around the table, on the phone, at work, at the beach, when we're out fishing – we all need to have our own conversations. I hope we can do that with respect and an open mind and open heart. I will be voting Yes. I hope you vote Yes but whatever you do, please do so with respect and remember that the Uluru Statement from the Heart is a call to all Australians and not just to the politicians or the leaders at the front. The call is made to you. I hope you can think about what the right thing to do is, not get bogged down in detail, and let us be heard – let this country truly sing with the spirit of more than 60,000 years.

Appendix

SOURCES AND FURTHER READING

ATSIC

www.aph.gov.au/Parliamentary_Business/Committees/Senate/Former_Committees/indigenousaffairs/report/final/c02

Bringing Them Home report

humanrights.gov.au/our-work/bringing-them-home-report-1997

Closing the Gap

closingthegap.gov.au/national-agreement

Indigenous Deaths in Custody

humanrights.gov.au/our-work/indigenous-deaths-custody-0

aic.gov.au/statistics/deaths-custody-australia

Out-of-home care

snaicc.org.au/media-release-number-of-aboriginal-and-torres-strait-islander-children-in-out-of-home-care-is-a-national-shame/

aihw.gov.au/news-media/media-releases/2021-1/may/rate-of-children-in-out-of-home-care-remains-stabl

absec.org.au

Race Power, Section 51(xxvi), the Australian Constitution

referendumcouncil.org.au/discussion-topics/amending-race-power.html

austlii.edu.au/au/journals/AUIndigLawRw/2011/18.pdf

The referendum on the Voice to Parliament

abc.net.au/news/voice-to-parliament-referendum

aec.gov.au/referendums/2023-referendum.htm

niaa.gov.au/indigenous-affairs/referendum-aboriginal-and-torres-strait-islander-voice

Stolen Generations
reconciliation.org.au/wp-content/uploads/2021/10/Lets-Talk...Apology.pdf

Uluru Statement from the Heart
ulurustatement.org

The Voice to Parliament
voice.gov.au
Indigenous Voice Co-design Process, Final Report to the Australian Government, July 2021. voice.gov.au/sites/default/files/resource/download/indigenous-voice-co-design-process-final-report_1.pdf

Yes 23 Campaign
yes23.com.au

If you would like to find out more about Hachette Australia, our authors, upcoming events and new releases, you can visit our website or our social media channels:

hachette.com.au

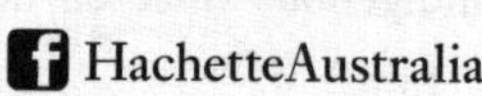

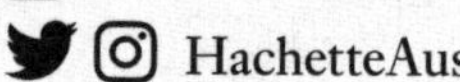